QUICK AND EASY

HAMLYN

COOK'S NOTES

OVEN TEMPERATURES

°C	°F	GAS MARK	
70 C	150 F	Low	–
80 C	175 F	Low	–
90 C	190 F	Low	–
100 C	200 F	¼	–
110 C	225 F	¼	Very slow
130 C	250 F	½	Very slow
150 C	275 F	1	Slow
160 C	300 F	2	Moderately slow
170 C	325 F	3	Moderately slow
180 C	350 F	4	Moderate
190 C	375 F	5	Moderately hot
200 C	400 F	6	Hot
220 C	425 F	7	Hot
230 C	450 F	8	Very hot
240 C	475 F	9	Very hot

MICROWAVE POWER SETTINGS

Power Level	Percentage	Numerical Setting
HIGH	100%	9
MEDIUM HIGH	75%	7
MEDIUM	50%	5
DEFROST	30%	3
LOW	10%	1

SOLID WEIGHT CONVERSIONS

METRIC	IMPERIAL
15 g	½ oz
25 g	1 oz
50 g	2 oz
100 g	4 oz/¼ lb
175 g	6 oz
225 g	8 oz/½ lb
350 g	12 oz
450 g	1 lb
575 g	1¼ lb
700 g	1½ lb
800 g	1¾ lb
900 g	2 lb

MICROWAVE

Microwave tips have been tested using a 650 watt microwave oven. Add 15 seconds per minute for 600 watt ovens and reduce the timings by 5-10 seconds per minute for 700 watt ovens.

LIQUID VOLUME CONVERSIONS

METRIC	IMPERIAL
25 ml	1 fl oz
50 ml	2 fl oz
125 ml	4 fl oz
150 ml	5 fl oz/¼ pt
175 ml	6 fl oz
225 ml	8 fl oz
300 ml	10 fl oz/½ pt
450 ml	15 fl oz/¾ pt
600 ml	20 fl oz/1pt
900 ml	1½ pt
1.2 l	2 pt
1.7 l	3 pt

AUSTRALIAN CUP CONVERSIONS

	METRIC	IMP
1 cup flour	150 g	5 oz
1 cup sugar, granulated	225 g	8 oz
1 cup sugar, caster	225 g	8 oz
1 cup sugar, icing	175 g	6 oz
1 cup sugar, soft brown	175 g	6 oz
1 cup butter	225 g	8 oz
1 cup honey, treacle	350 g	12 oz
1 cup fresh breadcrumbs	50 g	2 oz
1 cup uncooked rice	200 g	7 oz
1 cup dried fruit	175 g	6 oz
1 cup chopped nuts	100 g	4 oz
1 cup desiccated coconut	75 g	3 oz
1 cup liquid	250 ml	9 floz

WEIGHTS AND MEASURES

Metric and Imperial weights and measures are given throughout. Don't switch from one to the other within a recipe as they are not interchangeable. 1 tsp is the equivalent of a 5 ml spoon and 1 tbls equals a 15 ml spoon.

All spoon measurements are level, all flour plain, all sugar granulated and all eggs medium unless otherwise stated.

SYMBOLS

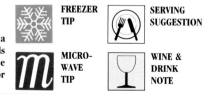

FREEZER TIP

SERVING SUGGESTION

MICRO-WAVE TIP

WINE & DRINK NOTE

CONTENTS

First published in Great Britain in 1993 by Hamlyn
an imprint of Reed Consumer Books Limited
Michelin House, 81 Fulham Road, London SW3 6RB
and Auckland, Melbourne, Singapore and Toronto

Reprinted 1993, 1994 (twice)

Copyright © GE Fabbri Limited 1993
Photographs and text copyright © GE Fabbri Limited 1988, 1989, 1993

ISBN 0 600 57772 4

A CIP catalogue record for this book is available from the British Library

Produced by Mandarin Offset
Printed and bound in Singapore

SAVOURY JACKET POTATOES

Paul Moon

Jacket potatoes provide a basis for a variety of tasty fillings. Each filling makes enough for four potatoes. Choose one and enjoy a really tasty and interesting snack.

PREPARATION TIME: 10-20 MINS
COOKING TIME: 1 1/4 HOURS
SERVES 4

INGREDIENTS

4 x 225 G/8 OZ BAKING POTATOES

25 G/1 OZ BUTTER

1-2 TBLS MILK

SALT AND GROUND BLACK PEPPER

FLAT-LEAVED PARSLEY, TO GARNISH

CHEESE AND ONION FILLING

25 G/1 OZ BUTTER

2 SPRING ONIONS, FINELY CHOPPED

50 G/2 OZ CHEDDAR CHEESE, GRATED

BACON AND MUSHROOM FILLING

25 G/1 OZ BUTTER

4 RASHERS OF BACON, CHOPPED

50 G/2 OZ MUSHROOMS, THINLY SLICED

2 TOMATOES, SLICED

2 EGGS, BEATEN

SALMON FILLING

60 G/2 1/2 OZ TINNED PINK SALMON

2 TBLS MAYONNAISE

1-2 TBLS TOMATO KETCHUP

SALT AND GROUND BLACK PEPPER

1 Preheat the oven to 200 C/400 F/ Gas 6. Prick the potatoes all over with a fork then bake for 1 hour, or until a skewer can be pushed easily into them. Cut the potatoes open, scoop out the centres, mash with the butter and milk and season with salt and pepper.

m PIERCE THE POTATOES, WRAP IN A DOUBLE THICKNESS OF KITCHEN PAPER AND COOK ON HIGH (100%) FOR 12-15 MINUTES. LEAVE POTATOES TO STAND FOR 3-4 MINUTES THEN SCOOP OUT CENTRES, PRE-PARE THE FILLING AND COOK FOR A FURTHER 3-5 MINUTES.

2 For the cheese and onion filling: place the butter and onions in a pan and cook until the onions are soft. Stir in the potato and half the cheese. Pile into the skins. Sprinkle with the remaining cheese and grill.

3 For the bacon and mushroom filling: melt the butter and cook the bacon and mushrooms for 5 minutes. Put half the potato mixture into the skins and add half the bacon, mushrooms and tomatoes. Put the remainder of the potato mixture into a piping bag and pipe a border around each potato. Fill the centres with the remaining bacon, mushrooms and tomatoes. Spoon the egg over the top and put potatoes back in the oven until heated through.

4 For the salmon filling: drain the salmon and discard any skin and bones. Mash with the potato, mayonnaise, tomato ketchup and seasoning. Pile into the skins, reheat in the oven, garnish and serve.

STUFFED AUBERGINES

Clint Brown

This purple, satin-skinned vegetable is ideal
for stuffing – and available all the year round.
Here the halves are filled with smoked ham
and bubbling cheese sauce.

PREPARATION TIME: 20 MINS
COOKING TIME: 45 MINS
SERVES 2

INGREDIENTS

| 2 MEDIUM AUBERGINES |
| 100 G/4 OZ SMOKED HAM |
| 75 ML/3 FL OZ OLIVE OIL |
| 40 G/1 ½ OZ BUTTER |
| 1 MEDIUM COURGETTE, SLICED |
| 25 G/1 OZ FLOUR |
| 300 ML/½ PT MILK |
| 50 G/2 OZ CHEDDAR, GRATED |
| 2 TSP CREAMED HORSERADISH SAUCE |
| SALT AND GROUND BLACK PEPPER |
| 4 TBLS FRESH WHITE BREADCRUMBS |
| 1 TBLS CHOPPED PARSLEY |
| 2 TBLS GRATED PARMESAN CHEESE |

1 Remove the stalks from the aubergines and slice them in half lengthways. Carefully scoop out the aubergine flesh without breaking the skin. Cut the flesh and ham into 12 mm/ ½ in cubes. Heat 3 tbls of oil in a heavy-based frying-pan. Add the aubergine shells and fry over a gentle heat until they start to soften. Drain on kitchen paper.

2 Add the remaining oil to the frying-pan, sauté the aubergine flesh for 5 minutes until lightly softened. Remove from the pan and drain on kitchen paper.

3 Melt 15 g/½ oz butter in a saucepan and cook the ham for 3-5 minutes. Add the courgette to the pan and sauté for 1 minute. Remove the ham and courgette with a spoon and add the remaining butter to the pan. When melted, stir in the flour and milk and bring to the boil, stirring continuously to make a smooth sauce. Stir in three-quarters of the Cheddar, the horseradish sauce and seasoning.

4 Preheat the oven to 200 C/400 F Gas 6. Mix together the aubergine flesh, ham and courgettes and spoon the mixture into the aubergine shells. Pour a little sauce over each then top with breadcrumbs mixed with the remaining Cheddar and parsley. Sprinkle with Parmesan. Bake near the top of the oven for 20-25 minutes or until golden.

 SERVE STUFFED AUBERGINES WITH SAUTE POTATOES AND A TOMATO SALAD.

 A RED WINE OR ROSE WOULD GO WELL WITH THIS DISH. TRY A CALIFORNIAN BURGUNDY OR MATEUS ROSE.

PASTA ALLA CARBONARA

Green and white tagliatelle gives a colourful base for this pasta dish. Use fresh pasta if you can get it.

PREPARATION TIME: 10 MINS
COOKING TIME: 10 MINS
SERVES 4

INGREDIENTS

225 G/8 OZ GREEN TAGLIATELLE

225 G/8 OZ WHITE TAGLIATELLE

SALT

2 TBLS OLIVE OIL

25 G/1 OZ BUTTER

175 G/6 OZ LEAN HAM, CUT INTO STRIPS

2 CLOVES OF GARLIC, CRUSHED

75 G/3 OZ FRESHLY GRATED PARMESAN CHEESE

3 EGG YOLKS

300 ML/½ PT DOUBLE CREAM

SALT AND GROUND BLACK PEPPER

TO SERVE

2 TBLS FRESHLY CHOPPED PARSLEY

GRATED PARMESAN CHEESE

1 Boil the tagliatelle in salted water. Drain and rinse thoroughly in hot water to remove surface starch. Drain again and return to the saucepan. Toss the pasta in the olive oil

2 Heat the butter and stir in the ham. Turn and cook quickly, then add the garlic and stir for a further minute. Add the ham and the garlic to the tagliatelle. Keep the pasta warm while you make the sauce.

3 Whisk together the Parmesan, egg yolks and cream. Season. Pour the mixture into a saucepan and stir over a low heat until it begins to thicken. Do not let the mixture boil or the cream will separate and eggs scramble.

4 Carefully stir the sauce and the pasta mixture together. Sprinkle with the chopped parsley and Parmesan cheese. Serve immediately.

SERVE THIS PASTA DISH WITH CRUSTY GARLIC BREAD AND A FENNEL AND LETTUCE SALAD.

PASTA WITH SPINACH SAUCE

Clint Brown

<u>Popeye may have popularised spinach, but this is one recipe he hasn't tried. With olive oil as an essential ingredient he'd be sure to love it!</u>

PREPARATION TIME: 5 MINS
COOKING TIME: 20 MINS
SERVES 4-6

INGREDIENTS

450 G/1 LB CHOPPED SPINACH,
THAWED IF FROZEN

225 G/8 OZ MASCARPONE CHEESE

25 G/1 OZ GROUND WALNUTS

6 TINNED ANCHOVIES

ANCHOVY OIL FROM THE TIN

SALT AND GROUND BLACK PEPPER

1 TSP GRATED NUTMEG

1 TBLS OLIVE OIL

250 G/9 OZ TAGLIATELLE

GRATED PARMESAN, TO SERVE

2 Bring a large pan of salted water to the boil with the olive oil. Add the pasta and boil, uncovered, for about 10 minutes. Drain well. Heat the sauce through gently and serve with the pasta and Parmesan.

WATCHPOINT

MAKE SURE YOU BUY THE RIGHT CHEESE FOR THIS RECIPE. MASCARPONE IS AN ITALIAN CREAM CHEESE WHICH IS INCREDIBLY SMOOTH — IT LOOKS LIKE SOLID DOUBLE CREAM.

1 Turn the chopped spinach into the bowl of a food processor and blend with the cheese, nuts, anchovies, anchovy oil, plenty of salt and black pepper and the nutmeg.

TIP

FOR A STRONGER FLAVOUR USE 3 BUNCHES OF FRESH WATERCRESS INSTEAD OF THE SPINACH. ADD 1 SAUTEED ONION, 2 CRUSHED GARLIC CLOVES AND BLEND WITH REMAINING INGREDIENTS AS ABOVE.

SAFFRON RISOTTO

This savoury rice dish is enriched by slices of
succulent mortadella sausage.

PREPARATION TIME: 10 MINS
COOKING TIME: 20 MINS
SERVES 6

INGREDIENTS

2 TBLS OLIVE OIL
1 ONION, CHOPPED
1 TSP OREGANO
350 G/12 OZ ARBORIO RICE
750 ML/1 ¼ PT CHICKEN STOCK
½ TSP SAFFRON STRANDS
150 ML/¼ PT WHITE WINE
350 G/12 OZ MORTADELLA SAUSAGE, SLICED INTO 6 MM/¼ IN PIECES
SALT AND GROUND BLACK PEPPER
75 G/3 OZ PARMESAN CHEESE, GRATED, TO SERVE

3 Turn out into a suitable serving bowl and serve with some freshly grated Parmesan cheese.

TIP

RISOTTOS SHOULD BE SERVED AS SOON AS THEY ARE COOKED OR THE RICE WILL LOSE ITS FIRM TEXTURE. ARBORIO RICE HAS AN OVAL-SHAPED GRAIN, AND IS SHORTER AND ROUNDER THAN AMERICAN SHORT GRAIN RICE.

WATCHPOINT

BE CAREFUL ONLY TO BUY PARMESAN CHEESE FROM A SHOP WHICH HAS A QUICK TURNOVER. PREFERABLY BUY A PIECE AND GRATE IT YOURSELF OTHERWISE IT BECOMES DRY AND LOSES ITS CREAMY PUNGENT FLAVOUR.

1 Heat the oil in a saucepan, add the onion and oregano. Cover and soften over a gentle heat.

2 Stir the arborio rice into the saucepan, add the chicken stock, the saffron strands (it is not necessary to soak them beforehand), white wine and the mortadella sausage strips. Season well with salt and ground black pepper. Bring to the boil and simmer, uncovered, for 17 minutes, or until all the liquid has been completely absorbed but the arborio rice is slightly firm in the middle.

SWORDFISH WITH TARTARE BUTTER

Dave Gill

This meaty fish is becoming widely available frozen from the fishmongers. If, however, you are unable to find it, use any firm-fleshed fish such as tuna, shark or halibut instead.

PREPARATION TIME: 20 MINS
COOKING TIME: 10 MINS
SERVES 4

INGREDIENTS

4 SWORDFISH STEAKS, THAWED IF
FROZEN

SALT AND GROUND BLACK PEPPER

1 TBLS MELTED BUTTER

SALAD LEAVES, TO SERVE

FOR THE TARTARE BUTTER

75 G/3 OZ BUTTER, SOFTENED

1 CLOVE OF GARLIC, CHOPPED

1 SHALLOT, FINELY CHOPPED

1 TBLS FINELY CHOPPED CAPERS

1 TBLS FINELY CHOPPED GHERKINS

1 TBLS FINELY CHOPPED FRESH
PARSLEY

3 DROPS OF WORCESTERSHIRE
SAUCE

3 DROPS OF TABASCO

SALT AND GROUND BLACK PEPPER

2 Heat the grill to high. Heat several metal skewers under the grill until very hot. Hold the end with a cloth and make a criss-cross pattern on one side of each steak. Heating several skewers at once speeds up the process.

3 Season the fish with salt and pepper. Brush each side with melted butter. Grill for 5 minutes on each side, brushing from time to time with the butter.

4 Remove the steaks from the grill and place on warmed serving plates. Remove the butter from the freezer and slice into four. Serve the fish with a slice of butter on top, and with the salad leaves.

1 First make the butter. Mix the softened butter with the garlic, shallot, capers, gherkins, parsley, Worcestershire sauce and Tabasco. Season with salt and pepper. Form into a fat sausage shape, wrap in greaseproof and put in the freezer for 20 minutes.

 SWORDFISH IS DELICIOUS SERVED WITH NEW POTATOES AND TOMATO SALAD.

TIP

THE STEAKS CAN BE MARKED IN A CRISS-CROSS PATTERN AFTER COOKING AS WELL — KEEP THE STEAKS WARM UNDER A LOW GRILL AS YOU MARK EACH ONE.

FISH KEBABS

James Duncan

Succulent cubes of white fish, some wrapped in bacon, are skewered to make a delightfully simple supper. Cod, coley and whiting are the right type of fish for this recipe.

PREPARATION TIME: 20 MINS
COOKING TIME: 10 MINS
SERVES 4

INGREDIENTS

450 G/1 LB FIRM WHITE FISH
FILLETS

4 RASHERS RINDLESS STREAKY
BACON

2 TBLS MELTED BUTTER

GROUND BLACK PEPPER

2 DILL FRONDS, CHOPPED

SALAD LETTUCE, TO GARNISH

1 Cut the fish into cubes. Lay the bacon on a chopping board and stretch by dragging the blade of a cook's knife along the surface, then cut into short lengths. Use the bacon to wrap half the fish chunks.

2 Skewer wrapped and plain fish alternately. Brush with butter, sprinkle with pepper and dill.

3 Heat the grill or barbecue to high. Grill the kebabs until barely brown, turning frequently. Scatter the remaining dill over the top and serve at once, garnished with the salad lettuce.

TIP

LEAVING THE SKIN ON WILL HELP HOLD THE CUBES OF FISH TOGETHER, BUT MAKE SURE IT IS FREE OF SCALES. KEEP THE SKIN ON THE OUTSIDE OF THE KEBAB SO IT CAN CRISP AND BROWN. IF PREFERRED, REMOVE THE SKIN BY PLACING FLESH-SIDE DOWN AND HOLDING THE SKIN TIGHTLY WHILST EASING THE FLESH AWAY WITH A KNIFE. DIPPING YOUR FINGERS IN SALT WILL GIVE YOU A FIRMER GRIP.

WATCHPOINT

THE KEBABS ARE QUITE DELICATE SO BRUSH THE GRILL-PAN WITH OIL TO PREVENT THEM FROM STICKING AND BREAKING. ALSO OIL OR GREASE THE SKEWERS BEFORE USING.

A WELL-CHILLED BOTTLE OF BLANC DE BLANCS WINE WILL COMPLEMENT THE DELICATE FLAVOUR OF THIS FISH DISH PERFECTLY.

PRAWN & CRAB CURRY

Chris King

This nutritious seafood curry is quick to prepare and cook and makes an excellent supper dish served on a bed of boiled rice.

PREPARATION TIME: 10 MINS
COOKING TIME: 15-20 MINS
SERVES 6

I N G R E D I E N T S

450 G/1 LB UNPEELED PRAWNS,
LARGE OR SMALL

1 ONION, FINELY SLICED

2 CLOVES OF GARLIC, CRUSHED

2 CHILLIES, SLICED

50 G/2 OZ BUTTER

1 TSP TURMERIC

1 TSP GROUND CORIANDER

2 TSP TOMATO PUREE

25 G/1 OZ CREAMED COCONUT

225 G/8 OZ CRAB CLAWS

JUICE OF 1 LIME

SALT

BOILED RICE, TO SERVE

50 G/2 OZ SHREDDED COCONUT,
TOASTED

2 Add the tomato purée, coconut and 175 ml/6 fl oz water. Bring to the boil, stirring, then add the prawns, crab and lime juice. Simmer the mixture gently for 10-15 minutes until the liquid thickens a little and the fish is heated right through.

3 Check the seasoning of the sauce. Add salt if required. Serve the curry over cooked rice, topped with shredded coconut.

TIP

FOR PERFECT RICE, MELT 25 G/1 OZ BUTTER IN A HEAVY-BASED OR NON-STICK SAUCEPAN AND SAUTE 275 G/10 OZ LONG GRAIN RICE FOR 1 MINUTE UNTIL THE GRAINS BEGIN TO LOOK SHINY. ADD 600 ML/1 PT OF BOILING WATER SEASONED WITH ½ TSP SALT AND BRING EVERY-THING TO THE BOIL. COVER, REDUCE THE HEAT TO LOW AND SIMMER THE RICE FOR 15 MINUTES. DO NOT BE TEMPTED TO LOOK AT IT DURING THIS TIME. UNCOVER AND FLUFF UP THE RICE WITH A FORK AND SERVE IMMEDIATELY.

1 Peel the prawns removing the heads, legs and body casing but retain the tail end on the prawn. Soften the onion, garlic and chillies in the butter for 3-4 minutes. Stir in the turmeric and coriander, cook for 2 minutes.

SERVE THIS PRAWN & CRAB CURRY WITH INDIAN POP-PADUMS.

LAGER OR ICED WATER IS USUALLY DRUNK WITH CURRY, BUT IF YOU WANT TO DRINK WINE, TRY GEWURZTRAMINER.

TOMATO & CAYENNE FISH CASSEROLE

Hilary Moore

This delicious, tomatoey fish dish is quick and easy to prepare and cook. Treat yourself to a taste of sunshine, warmth and a trouble-free meal.

PREPARATION TIME: 5 MINS
COOKING TIME: 15 MINS
SERVES 4

INGREDIENTS

1 LARGE ONION
1 TBLS OLIVE OIL
400 G/14 OZ TINNED CHOPPED TOMATOES
2 TBLS FRESH CHOPPED PARSLEY
½ TSP CAYENNE PEPPER
SALT AND GROUND BLACK PEPPER
2 COURGETTES, SLICED
4 GREY MULLET STEAKS

3 Add the courgettes and fish steaks to the pan, return to the boil, cover and simmer for 10 minutes or until the fish is cooked. Transfer to serving plates or a dish and serve.

TIP

IF MULLET STEAKS ARE DIFFICULT TO FIND, CHOOSE OTHER LARGE FISH STEAKS, SUCH AS COD, HADDOCK OR HALIBUT, AS AN ALTERNATIVE.

SERVE THIS CASSEROLE WITH PLAINLY BOILED WHITE, OR BROWN, RICE. ALTERNATIVELY, CRUSTY FRENCH OR GREEK BREAD AND BUTTER, TO MOP UP THE JUICES, WOULD BE EVEN QUICKER TO PREPARE. NO EXTRA VEGETABLES WILL BE NEEDED.

1 Slice the onion. Heat the oil in a frying-pan and fry the onion until tender but not browned.

2 Add the tomatoes, parsley and seasonings. Stir well, bring to the boil and cook for 2-3 minutes.

COCONUT PRAWNS

Peter Reilly

Prawns in coconut milk makes a delicious
- if rather rich - starter. It is very typical
of Southern Indian cooking.

PREPARATION TIME: 10 MINS
COOKING TIME: 16-25 MINS
SERVES 4

I N G R E D I E N T S

6 TBLS VEGETABLE OIL

10 FRESH CURRY LEAVES, OR USE
DRIED, CRUSHED CURRY LEAVES

1 ONION, FINELY SLICED

4 CLOVES OF GARLIC, THINLY SLICED

2.5 CM/1 IN PIECE OF FRESH ROOT
GINGER, PEELED AND FINELY
CHOPPED

1 TBLS PAPRIKA

PINCH OF CHILLI POWDER

1 TSP TURMERIC

2 TBLS GROUND CORIANDER

¼ TSP GROUND FENUGREEK

GROUND BLACK PEPPER

1 TBLS TAMARIND PASTE
(OR LEMON JUICE)

450 G/1 LB COOKED, PEELED
PRAWNS

300 ML/½ PT COCONUT MILK

CORIANDER, TO GARNISH

CURRY LEAVES, TO GARNISH

the mixture burn. Add the ginger, all the spices and pepper. Stir in the tamarind paste dissolved in 150 ml/¼ pt water.

2 Bring the contents of the pan to the boil, then reduce the heat and simmer for 5-10 minutes to reduce the cooking liquid. Add the prawns and stir for a further 5 minutes. Stir in the coconut milk and cook for a final 3-5 minutes. Garnish and serve.

TIP

IF YOU CAN ONLY GET TAMARIND IN A BLOCK, BREAK OFF A SECTION, SOAK IT IN HOT WATER FOR 10 MINUTES AND THEN SIEVE TO MAKE PASTE.

 THIS DISH IS DELICIOUS SERVED WITH WARMED CHA-PATIS OR NAAN BREAD, TOGETHER WITH A BOWL OF CHILLED RAITA.

1 Heat the oil in a very large frying-pan and add the fresh or dried curry leaves, finely sliced onion and fine slices of garlic. Cook for approximately 3-5 minutes, until they have turned golden brown. Take care not to let

ITALIAN RISOTTO

Simon Wheeler

Make this classic rice dish, finished in the Italian way with freshly grated Parmesan cheese and olive oil. Served in smaller amounts, risotto makes a good side dish.

PREPARATION TIME: 10 MINS
COOKING TIME: 25-30 MINS
SERVES 4-6

INGREDIENTS

50 G/2 OZ BUTTER
1 ONION, SLICED
2 CLOVES OF GARLIC, CRUSHED
100 G/4 OZ COURGETTES, SLICED
225 G/8 OZ LONG-GRAIN RICE
900 ML/1 ½ PT CHICKEN STOCK
PINCH OF SAFFRON
225 G/8 OZ PEELED PRAWNS
25 G/1 OZ GRATED PARMESAN CHEESE
1 TBLS OLIVE OIL

2 Add a third of the stock and the saffron to the vegetables and rice. Simmer gently until the rice absorbs the liquid. Add another third of the stock and simmer until all the liquid has been absorbed completely.

1 Heat the butter in a heavy-based frying-pan. Add the onion and fry for 3-4 minutes until softened. Add the garlic and courgettes and fry for a further 2 minutes. Add the rice and cook, stirring continuously, for 2 minutes.

3 Mix in the prawns and continue to cook until the rice is tender and moist, add extra stock if it needs it. Stir in the Parmesan cheese and oil, and transfer to a warmed serving dish.

TIP

USE AUTHENTIC ITALIAN ARBORIO RICE INSTEAD OF LONG-GRAIN. YOU CAN ALSO SUBSTITUTE 125 ML/4 FL OZ DRY WHITE WINE FOR SOME OF THE STOCK.

A BOTTLE OF CHILLED VEN-ETO, AN ITALIAN WHITE WINE, GOES WELL WITH THIS DISH.

TUNA LASAGNE

All the family will enjoy Tuna Lasagne. It can be prepared in advance then cooked in the oven without any fuss.

Nick Carmen

PREPARATION TIME: 15 MINS
COOKING TIME: 1 HOUR
SERVES 6

I N G R E D I E N T S

BUTTER, FOR GREASING
175 G/6 OZ QUICK-COOK LASAGNE
6 TOMATOES, SLICED
50 G/2 OZ CHEDDAR CHEESE, GRATED
FOR THE SAUCE
50 G/2 OZ BUTTER
1 ONION, FINELY CHOPPED
50 G/2 OZ FLOUR
600 ML/1 PT MILK
SALT AND GROUND BLACK PEPPER
½ TSP MUSTARD
1 TSP WORCESTERSHIRE SAUCE
175 G/6 OZ CHEDDAR CHEESE, GRATED
400 G/14 OZ TINNED TUNA, DRAINED AND SHREDDED

2 Remove from the heat and stir in the milk. Season with salt and pepper then return the pan to the heat and cook, stirring constantly until the sauce coats the back of the spoon. Stir in the mustard, Worcestershire sauce, cheese and tuna and cook for a further 2 minutes.

3 Grease a medium-sized ovenproof dish with the butter. Place a layer of tuna sauce on the bottom of the dish. Cover with a layer of lasagne, another layer of tuna sauce and then a layer of tomatoes. Continue making layers in this way, ending with a layer of tuna sauce. Reserve a few sliced tomatoes for the top.

1 Preheat the oven to 180 C/350 F/ Gas 4. Make the sauce: melt the butter in a large saucepan. Add the finely chopped onion and cook for 4-5 minutes or until golden in colour. Sprinkle in the flour and cook, stirring constantly for 2 minutes.

4 Sprinkle the grated Cheddar cheese over the top, garnish with the remaining sliced tomatoes and cover with foil. Bake for 25 minutes, then remove the foil and bake for a further 15-20 minutes or until the top is golden brown.

 SERVE WITH A CRISP GREEN SALAD AND SOME WARM FRENCH BREAD.

 THIS DISH IS IDEAL FOR FREEZING. THAW OVERNIGHT BEFORE COOKING.

TROUT WITH HAZELNUTS

Clint Brown

Low in fat and high in protein, trout is delicious and very versatile. Serve it with this nutty dill sauce for a fast but impressive main dish.

PREPARATION TIME: 20 MINS
COOKING TIME: 15 MINS
SERVES 4

I N G R E D I E N T S

4 x 225 G/8 OZ RAINBOW TROUT

SALT AND GROUND BLACK PEPPER

25 G/1 OZ BUTTER

1 TBLS OIL

75 G/3 OZ HAZELNUTS, SKINNED

2 TBLS WHITE WINE VINEGAR

2 LARGE EGG YOLKS

225 G/8 OZ UNSALTED BUTTER, MELTED

1-2 TBLS CHOPPED FRESH DILL

LEMON SLICES, TO GARNISH

SPRIGS OF DILL, TO GARNISH

3 Reduce the vinegar to 1 tbls in a pan. Cool. Roast and chop the remaining nuts. Tip yolks and vinegar into a food processor.

4 Slowly pour the unsalted butter through the funnel onto the egg mixture until thick. Add chopped hazelnuts and dill. Season.

1 Clean trout cavities with salt. Melt the butter and oil in a large heavy-based pan. Gently fry the trout on each side for 5-6 minutes until golden brown and cooked through.

2 Remove the trout from the frying-pan and keep hot. Divide the hazelnuts and add half to pan. Fry until golden brown. Drain well on kitchen paper and keep warm.

5 Garnish fish with lemon slices, sprigs of dill and whole nuts. Gently warm the hazelnut sauce and serve separately.

TIP

NUTS CAN BECOME STALE VERY QUICKLY SO ONLY BUY SMALL QUANTITIES AND ALWAYS KEEP IN AN AIRTIGHT TIN.

 SERVE THESE RAINBOW TROUT WITH MANGETOUT OR A GREEN SALAD AND PLENTY OF SAUTEED POTATOES.

SHRIMP PILAFF

Peter Reilly

Variations on the theme of rice and stock abound, but this tasty shrimp dish is one of the best.

PREPARATION TIME: 15 MINS
COOKING TIME: 15-20 MINS
SERVES 4

I N G R E D I E N T S

1 LARGE ONION, CHOPPED
2 STICKS OF CELERY, CHOPPED
1 CLOVE OF GARLIC, CRUSHED
1 LARGE CARROT, FINELY DICED
2 TBLS OLIVE OIL
225 G/8 OZ LONG-GRAIN RICE
SALT AND GROUND BLACK PEPPER
LARGE PINCH OF SAFFRON STRANDS
900 ML/1 ½ PT VEGETABLE STOCK
1 TSP CHOPPED FRESH BASIL
2 x 400 G/14 OZ TINNED SHRIMPS, DRAINED
SPRIGS FRESH BASIL, TO GARNISH

2 Add the rice, seasoning, saffron strands and the stock. Bring to the boil, cover and simmer for 10-15 minutes until the rice is tender and all the liquid has been completely absorbed.

1 Cook the onion, celery, garlic and carrot in the olive oil until tender and golden brown.

3 Add the basil and shrimps, adjust the seasoning according to taste and serve after stirring with a wooden spoon to separate the grains. Garnish with the sprigs of basil.

 PLACE THE VEGETABLES AND OIL IN A LARGE MICROWAVE-PROOF BOWL. COVER AND COOK ON HIGH (100%) FOR 4 MINUTES STIRRING TWICE. ADD RICE, SEASONING, SAFFRON STRANDS AND STOCK, COVER AND COOK FOR 10-12 MINUTES. ADD SHRIMPS AND BASIL, COVER AND COOK FOR 2 MINUTES.

CORONATION CHICKEN

Clint Brown

A dish specially invented for the Queen's Coronation in 1953. This modern version uses fresh mango and mango chutney instead of the apricots used in the original recipe.

PREPARATION TIME: 20 MINS
SERVES 4-6

INGREDIENTS

1 LARGE FIRM RIPE MANGO
50 G/2 OZ SULTANAS
1 KG/2 LB 4 OZ CHICKEN BREAST, COOKED, SKINNED AND CUT INTO 12 MM/½ IN STRIPS
150 ML/¼ PT MAYONNAISE
1-1½ TSP MILD CURRY POWDER
1 TBLS MANGO CHUTNEY
1 TSP LEMON JUICE
SALT AND GROUND BLACK PEPPER
100 G/4 OZ CASHEW NUTS, TOASTED

3 Mix the mayonnaise with the curry powder, chutney and lemon juice. Season. Pour over the chicken mixture and toss gently. Add half the nuts and mix in well.

4 Transfer to a serving dish and garnish with the remaining mango strips and cashew nuts.

TIP

IF YOU CHOP THE MANGO AND THE CHICKEN INTO SMALLER PIECES THIS MAKES A DELICIOUS, MOIST SANDWICH FILLING FOR A PACKED LUNCH.

SERVE WITH A RICE SALAD OR ARRANGED ON A BED OF CRISPY GREEN SALAD.

1 Remove the skin from the mango. Chop the flesh off either side of the stone, and slice into strips.

2 Put half of the mango strips, sultanas, and the chicken in a large bowl.

CHINESE CHICKEN & CASHEWS

Clint Brown

A quick and easy Chinese dish with a medley of flavours and textures which will make you come back for more. Serve with boiled rice or noodles.

PREPARATION TIME: 15 MINS
COOKING TIME: 20 MINS
SERVES 4

INGREDIENTS

4 SKINLESS CHICKEN BREASTS
2 CARROTS
1 GREEN PEPPER
425 G/15 OZ TINNED PINEAPPLE PIECES, IN NATURAL JUICE
2 TBLS PEANUT OIL
225 G/8 OZ TINNED WATER-CHESTNUTS, HALVED
100 G/4 OZ CASHEW NUTS
2 TBLS DARK SOY SAUCE
2 TBLS DRY SHERRY
1 TBLS MALT VINEGAR
1 TBLS CORNFLOUR
½ TSP GROUND GINGER
SALT AND GROUND BLACK PEPPER

2 Heat the peanut oil and fry the chicken for 5 minutes, then add carrots, pepper, pineapple, water-chestnuts and cashew nuts. Stir-fry for 5 minutes.

3 Mix together soy sauce, sherry, vinegar and pineapple juice. Blend in cornflour and ginger. Pour the sauce over meat and vegetables, bring to the boil, stirring until thickened. Cover and simmer for 10 minutes. Season with salt and pepper and serve.

1 Cut chicken, carrots and green pepper into 1 cm/⅓ in strips. Drain pineapple, reserving juice.

 COOK CHICKEN COVERED ON HIGH (100%) FOR 6 MINUTES. COOK VEGETABLES, PINEAPPLE AND NUTS IN OIL ON HIGH (100%) FOR 5 MINUTES. ADD CHICKEN, SAUCE INGREDIENTS, COVER AND COOK ON HIGH FOR 8 MINUTES.

FRIED CHICKEN & CORN FRITTERS

Clint Brown

Chicken is cheap but not always cheerful – so spice it up with this southern-style crispy coating and serve with golden corn fritters. Guaranteed to fill up the greediest of guests!

**PREPARATION TIME: 20 MINS
+ CHILLING
COOKING TIME: 30-35 MINS
SERVES 6**

INGREDIENTS

1.4 KG/3 LB OVEN-READY CHICKEN
CUT INTO 6 PORTIONS

300 ML/½ PT MILK

¼ TSP CAYENNE PEPPER

½ TSP PAPRIKA

225 G/8 OZ SEASONED FLOUR

OIL, FOR SHALLOW FRYING

400 G/14 OZ TINNED SWEETCORN

1 RED PEPPER, CHOPPED

100 G/4 OZ FLOUR

50 ML/2 FL OZ MILK

1 TSP BAKING POWDER

2 EGGS, LIGHTLY BEATEN

SALT AND GROUND BLACK PEPPER

1 TBLS BUTTER, MELTED

SALAD, TO SERVE

1 Dip the chicken portions in the milk. Mix the cayenne pepper and paprika with the flour. Coat the chicken. Chill for 30 minutes.

2 Heat the oil in a large frying-pan. Shallow fry each chicken portion for 10-12 minutes until crisp and golden. Drain on kitchen paper and keep warm in the oven.

3 To make the fritters: mix together the sweetcorn, red pepper, flour, milk, baking powder, eggs and seasoning. Stir in the melted butter.

4 Heat more oil in a large frying-pan. Drop in tablespoonfuls of the batter, a few at a time. Fry for 5 minutes, turning occasionally until golden. Remove with a slotted spoon and drain on kitchen paper. Repeat this process until you have used all the batter. Serve with the chicken portions.

TIP

ADD MORE COLOUR TO THE FRITTERS BY ADDING CHOPPED GREEN PEPPERS TO THE BATTER MIXTURE.

LIME MARINATED CHICKEN

Clint Brown

The tropical zing of a sublime marinade gives this chicken dish such a lift that you'll think you're on an exotic holiday.

PREPARATION TIME: 20 MINS
+ MARINATING
COOKING TIME: 30-35 MINS
SERVES 4

I N G R E D I E N T S

4 CHICKEN BREASTS PORTIONS
GRATED ZEST AND JUICE OF 3 LIMES
PINCH OF SAFFRON
40 G/1 ½ OZ BUTTER
1 TBLS OLIVE OIL
25 G/1 OZ FLAKED ALMONDS
2 TBLS ACACIA BLOSSOM HONEY
1 TSP FRESHLY CHOPPED THYME
2 TBLS FRESHLY CHOPPED MINT
SALT AND GROUND BLACK PEPPER
MINT SPRIG, TO GARNISH

1 Prick the chicken all over with a skewer. Marinate in the lime zest, juice and saffron for at least 24 hours, turning the chicken frequently.

2 Melt 25 g/1 oz of the butter with the oil in a pan. Remove the chicken from the marinade with a slotted spoon. Add the chicken to the pan and fry until golden. Remove and set aside. Add the almonds and fry until golden. Remove and drain off the fat.

3 Stir the honey into the marinade. Return the chicken breasts and almonds to the pan. Add the chopped thyme, half the chopped mint and season with the salt and pepper. Pour the marinade over the chicken in the pan. Add the remaining butter. Tightly cover the pan and simmer for 20-30 minutes until the chicken is tender.

4 Put the chicken onto a warmed serving dish and spoon over the pan juices and almonds and sprinkle over rest of the chopped mint. Garnish with a sprig of mint.

SERVE WITH NEW POTATOES AND A FRESH GREEN SALAD OR MIXED VEGETABLES.

TURKEY & LIVER IN BASIL SAUCE

Clint Brown

Rich chicken livers combine with turkey breast to make this dish a feast to remember at any time of year.

PREPARATION TIME: 20 MINS
COOKING TIME: 15-20 MINS
SERVES 4

I N G R E D I E N T S

700 G/1 LB 8 OZ TURKEY
BREAST MEAT

50 G/2 OZ BUTTER

75 G/3 OZ CHICKEN LIVERS, CUT INTO
PIECES

100 G/4 OZ OYSTER MUSHROOMS,
SLICED

75 ML/3 FL OZ BRANDY

125 ML/4 FL OZ CHICKEN STOCK

8 G/¼ OZ BASIL LEAVES, SLICED
THINLY

300 ML/½ PT DOUBLE CREAM

SALT AND GROUND WHITE PEPPER

3 Stir in the mushrooms. Pour over the brandy and ignite. Allow the flames to die down, then add the chicken stock. Simmer to reduce the stock and juices by half.

1 Cut the turkey breast into strips and cook in a frying-pan with the butter, stirring until the meat is lightly browned.

4 Add the shredded basil leaves and cream. Bring to the boil, season and simmer for a further 2-3 minutes then serve immediately.

YOU NEED SOMETHING TO MOP UP THE WONDERFUL JUICES, SO SERVE WITH WILD RICE OR CREAMED POTATOES WITH A HINT OF NUTMEG, AND FRESH GREEN VEGETABLES, SUCH AS MANGETOUT. GARNISH WITH SMALL SPRIGS OF FRESH BASIL OR PARSLEY.

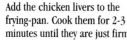

2 Add the chicken livers to the frying-pan. Cook them for 2-3 minutes until they are just firm.

SHREDDED CHICKEN STIR-FRY

Andrew Whittuck

All you need for this recipe are some everyday ingredients and a wok or large frying-pan for stir-frying. Served in bowls, these bite-sized pieces are ideal when you want to try your hand at chop-sticks.

PREPARATION TIME: 30 MINS
COOKING TIME: 3 MINS
SERVES 4

INGREDIENTS

4 CHICKEN BREASTS, SKINNED

½ A CUCUMBER

PINCH OF SALT

½ A GREEN PEPPER

6 SPRING ONIONS

1 TBLS OIL

¼ TSP CHILLI POWDER

2 CLOVES OF GARLIC, CRUSHED

2 TSP LIGHT SOY SAUCE

2 TSP DRY SHERRY

1 TSP RUNNY HONEY

colander, sprinkle with salt and set aside to drain for 20 minutes.

3 Slice the pepper into thin strips and cut the spring onions lengthways into pieces the same size as the cucumber. Rinse the cucumber well and pat dry with kitchen paper.

Ian O'Leary

4 Heat the oil in a wok or frying-pan and when hot add the green pepper and stir-fry for 30 seconds. Add the chicken and stir-fry for 1 minute or until the chicken is firm and cooked through. Add the chilli powder and spring onions and stir-fry for 30 seconds, then add the cucumber and garlic. Fry for another 30 seconds, add the soy sauce, sherry and honey. Serve immediately.

1 Cut the chicken breasts into thin shreds about 7.5 cm/3 in long, using a sharp knife.

2 Cut the cucumber in half lengthways, then into three widthways. Remove the seeds with a teaspoon. Slice each piece into narrow strips, 6 mm/¼ in wide. Put them in a

TIP

THE SECRET TO SUCCESSFUL STIR-FRYING IS TO WAIT UNTIL THE OIL IS VERY HOT AND THEN TO STIR CONSTANTLY SO THE INGREDIENTS THAT ARE USED REMAIN CRISP AND FIRM.

 FOR A MORE SUBSTANTIAL MEAL SERVE THIS DISH WITH SWEET & SOUR VEGETABLES.

BARBEQUED LAMB

Alan Marsh

Succulent leg of lamb flavoured with red wine
and parsley makes an interesting variation
to the more usual barbequed beef.

PREPARATION TIME: 10 MINS
+ MARINATING
COOKING TIME: 12-15 MINS
SERVES 8

I N G R E D I E N T S

8 LEG OF LAMB STEAKS

FRESH CHOPPED PARSLEY, TO
GARNISH

FOR THE MARINADE

1 LEMON

150 ML/¼ PT RED WINE

50 ML/2 FL OZ OLIVE OIL

2 CLOVES OF GARLIC, CRUSHED

5 TBLS CHOPPED FRESH PARSLEY

SALT AND GROUND BLACK PEPPER

3 Place the lamb in the marinade, ensuring that each steak is well coated. Cover and marinate in the fridge for at least two hours.

4 To cook, drain the steaks of excess marinade and place over a hot barbecue – 12 minutes for medium and 15 minutes for well done, turning and basting frequently. Sprinkle with chopped parsley and remaining lemon strips.

WATCHPOINT

MAKE SURE THAT THE BARBECUE COALS ARE VERY HOT BEFORE ADDING THE STEAKS TO THE GRID, OR YOU MAY FIND THE MEAT WILL BECOME DRY AND TOUGH.

1 Using a zester or vegetable peeler, remove the zest from the lemon and cut it into fine shreds.

2 Cut lemon in half and squeeze the juice into a large flat dish. Add half the zest strips and remaining marinade ingredients. Mix well.

LAMB & PEACH PARCELS

Dave Gill

Bite into the crispy coating of these neat little parcels to discover succulent pieces of lamb and a peachy stuffing.

PREPARATION TIME: 15 MINS
+ SOAKING
COOKING TIME: 20 MINS
SERVES 4

INGREDIENTS

1 ONION, CHOPPED
60 G/2½ OZ BUTTER
50 G/2 OZ DRIED PEACHES, SOAKED OVERNIGHT AND CHOPPED
1 TBLS FRESH CHOPPED DILL
2 CLOVES OF GARLIC, CRUSHED
50 G/2 OZ BREADCRUMBS
SALT AND GROUND BLACK PEPPER
1 EGG, BEATEN
700 G/1 LB 8 OZ BEST END OF NECK OF LAMB, BONED AND SKINNED
OIL, FOR FRYING
FOR THE COATING
4 TBLS SEASONED FLOUR
2 EGGS, BEATEN
50 G/2 OZ FRESH BREADCRUMBS

2 Open out the lamb and place fat side down on a surface. Spread the stuffing over the lamb and roll up. Secure with 8 lengths of string at even intervals along the roll. Using a sharp knife, cut through the meat in between the string to give 8 noisettes.

3 Push a cocktail stick through each noisette to secure the meat, then cut off the string. Coat each noisette in the seasoned flour, then the egg and then the breadcrumbs.

1 In a pan, soften the onion in 15 g/½ oz of the butter until transparent. Mix the peaches, dill, garlic and breadcrumbs together, then stir in the onions and seasoning. Add the beaten egg, a little at a time, until the stuffing is bound together.

SERVE WITH BABY SWEET-CORN, BROCCOLI, NEW POTA-TOES SPRINKLED WITH MINT AND CRUSTY BREAD.

4 Heat the remaining butter and the oil and add the noisettes. Fry for 4-6 minutes on each side over a moderate heat. If frying in batches, keep the noisettes warm in oven. Drain them well on kitchen paper and serve.

HONEY-GLAZED LAMB CHOPS

Michael Michaels

Lamb chops served with minty courgette
ribbons will appeal to all the family.

PREPARATION TIME: 10 MINS
COOKING TIME: 20-25 MINS
SERVES 4

INGREDIENTS

SALT AND GROUND BLACK PEPPER

4 LOIN LAMB CHOPS

4 TBLS RUNNY HONEY

2 TBLS SOY SAUCE

225 G/8 OZ COURGETTES, TRIMMED

25 G/1 OZ BUTTER

2 TBLS MINT JELLY

SPRIGS OF MINT, TO GARNISH

MINT JELLY, TO SERVE

3 Meanwhile, peel the courgettes lengthways into long, thin ribbons, using a potato peeler. Blanch the ribbons for about 2 minutes in boiling water. Drain and set aside.

4 Melt the butter and mint jelly in a saucepan. Then toss in the courgette ribbons and continue to toss until they are evenly coated. Remove from the pan while still crisp. Serve the courgette ribbons with the honey-glazed lamb chops. Garnish with mint and serve mint jelly in a separate dish.

TIP

TO PREVENT CHOPS FROM GOING OUT OF SHAPE, TRIM THE FAT OFF AND SECURE THE CHOPS NEATLY BY INSERTING A COCKTAIL STICK TO CONNECT THE TAIL-END OF THE CHOP TO THE MEATY PART BEFORE COOKING, BUT REMEMBER TO REMOVE THE STICKS BEFORE SERVING.

1 Preheat the grill to medium heat. Season the chops on both sides. Cover the grill pan with foil and lay the lamb chops on top. Mix together the honey and soy sauce, then use to brush over the chops on one side.

2 Grill the chops for 5-10 minutes then turn them over and baste on the other side. Continue to grill, basting the chops frequently with the juices, until the meat is cooked and the chops are nicely glazed.

HONEY-GLAZED LAMB CHOPS ARE COMPLEMENTED BY A GLASS OF MEDIUM-BODIED VALPOLICELLA, A RED ITALIAN WINE, WHICH COMES FROM NEAR VERONA.

GAMMON IN APPLE SAUCE

Nick Carman

The slightly sharp apple and mustard sauce complements the flavour of gammon. Gammon can be bought as steaks or you can cut your own off a joint.

PREPARATION TIME: 10 MINS
COOKING TIME: 10-20 MINS
SERVES 4

I N G R E D I E N T S

| 4 GAMMON STEAKS, TRIMMED |
| 1 TBLS CLEAR HONEY |
| 2 TBLS WINE VINEGAR |
| 1 TBLS WHOLEGRAIN MUSTARD |
| 2 TBLS CORNFLOUR |
| SALT AND GROUND BLACK PEPPER |
| 600 ML/1 PT APPLE JUICE |
| 2 GREEN APPLES |
| 25 G/1 OZ BUTTER |

2 Meanwhile blend the honey, wine vinegar, mustard, cornflour and seasoning together in a saucepan. Gradually pour the apple juice into the pan, stirring constantly, until it is well blended. Bring to the boil, stirring until the sauce thickens, then remove the saucepan from the heat.

1 Preheat the grill. Snip the gammon steaks with scissors around the edges at 2.5 cm/1 in intervals, then grill for 5-10 minutes on each side until tender.

THIS IS DELICIOUS SERVED WITH MASHED POTATO AND SHREDDED CABBAGE. AS AN ALTERNATIVE, SERVE THE SAUCE AND APPLE GARNISH WITH GRILLED, OR PAN-FRIED PORK CHOPS OR WITH TENDER LAMB STEAKS.

3 Halve the apples and core, then cut each half into pieces. Fry the apples in the butter until golden. Place the gammon steaks on warmed serving plates. Spoon over the sauce and serve with the apple pieces.

THE SAUCE CAN BE MADE IN ADVANCE AND FROZEN FOR UP TO 6 MONTHS. THAW THE SAUCE BEFORE REHEATING GENTLY IN A SAUCEPAN.

GAMMON WITH PLUM SAUCE

Clint Brown

Gammon steaks are quick to prepare and have no wastage. Bring out the flavour of the meat with this tasty and unusual sauce and serve with a bottle of sparkling rosé wine.

PREPARATION TIME: 10 MINS
COOKING TIME: 20 MINS
SERVES 4

I N G R E D I E N T S

4 LARGE GAMMON STEAKS

175 G/6 OZ TINNED RED PLUMS,
DRAINED AND STONED

1 TBLS PLUM SYRUP (RESERVED
PLUM JUICE)

50 G/2 OZ CASTER SUGAR

1 TBLS FRESHLY CHOPPED MIXED
HERBS

FOR THE GARNISH

FRESH PARSLEY SPRIGS

3 Press the mixture through a sieve and return the purée to the saucepan. Add the caster sugar and bring to the boil. Reduce the heat and simmer for 10 minutes until the sauce thickens. Stir in the chopped herbs.

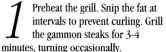

4 Pour the plum sauce over the gammon steaks. Garnish with parsley and serve immediately.

 GAMMON STEAKS ARE DELI-CIOUS SERVED WITH AN ACCOMPANIMENT OF COOKED BROCCOLI TOSSED IN BUTTER AND MASHED POTATOES.

 SERVE THIS DISH WITH A BOTTLE OF D'ANJOU, A FRENCH ROSE.

1 Preheat the grill. Snip the fat at intervals to prevent curling. Grill the gammon steaks for 3-4 minutes, turning occasionally.

2 Mix the plums, plum syrup and 150 ml/¼ pt water in a saucepan and bring to the boil. Stir continuously for 1-2 minutes, using a wooden spoon to break up the plum flesh.

PIPERADE

This well-known dish of peppers and eggs comes from the Basque region and is one of the most widely travelled of all French recipes.

PREPARATION TIME: 10 MINS
COOKING TIME: 45 MINS
SERVES 4

I N G R E D I E N T S

3 RED PEPPERS
3 TBLS OLIVE OIL
3 ONIONS, CHOPPED
2 CLOVES OF GARLIC, CHOPPED
1 FRESH RED CHILLI, SEEDED AND CHOPPED
900 G/2 LB TOMATOES, SKINNED, SEEDED AND CHOPPED
SALT AND FRESHLY GROUND BLACK PEPPER
6 EGGS, BEATEN
BASIL LEAVES, TO GARNISH
BAYONNE HAM, TO SERVE

3 Add the chopped tomatoes and season with salt and pepper. Cook for 15-20 minutes, over a low heat, stirring frequently until most of the moisture has evaporated and the mixture is a thick purée.

1 Preheat the oven to 230 C/450 F/ Gas 8. Place the peppers on a baking tray and bake them for 10-15 minutes, until they are slightly charred. Remove the skins from the peppers with a sharp knife, then seed and cut them into thin strips.

4 Gradually stir the beaten eggs into the vegetable mixture and return to the heat for 3-4 minutes, until the eggs are cooked through but still soft and creamy. Taste and adjust the seasoning, if necessary. Transfer to a serving dish, garnish with the fresh basil leaves and serve the Pipérade topped with Bayonne ham.

2 Heat the olive oil in a large frying-pan. Add the onions and cook over a low heat for 5 minutes, until they are softened. Stir in the skinned red peppers, chopped cloves of garlic and seeded and chopped chilli and cook for a further 5 minutes.

TIP

THIS DISH MUST BE COOKED SLOWLY UNTIL ALL THE MOISTURE HAS EVAPORATED BEFORE ADDING THE EGGS. LIGHTLY GRILLED BACK BACON RASHERS OR GAMMON RASHERS CAN BE SERVED, IF BAYONNE HAM IS UNAVAILABLE.

BEEF & ORANGE STIR-FRY

Andrew Whittuck

Tender strips of beef need only a couple of minutes in the pan to get a distinctive Chinese flavour. Serve this saucy orange beef on boiled noodles or rice for a speedy Chinese meal.

PREPARATION TIME: 25 MINS
COOKING TIME: 5 MINS
SERVES 4

INGREDIENTS

350 G/12 OZ LEAN RUMP BEEF
1 ORANGE
2½ TBLS VEGETABLE OIL
¼ TSP HOT CHILLI POWDER
1 TSP DARK SOY SAUCE
1 TSP SOFT BROWN SUGAR
½ TSP SESAME OIL
BOILED NOODLES, TO SERVE
FOR THE MARINADE
2 TSP DARK SOY SAUCE
12 MM/½ IN PIECE OF FRESH GINGER, PEELED AND DICED
2 TSP DRY SHERRY
1 TSP CORNFLOUR
1 TSP SESAME OIL

1 Cut the beef across the grain into strips, 5 cm/2 in long and the thickness of a pencil.

2 Next make the marinade: put the dark soy sauce into a mixing bowl. Add the strips of beef and then add the very finely diced root ginger, dry sherry, the cornflour and sesame oil. Stir the mixture until well blended and leave at room temperature to marinate for about 20 minutes.

3 Meanwhile, pare the zest from half the orange being sure not to remove any of the bitter white pith. Cut these strips lengthways into fine shreds and blanch in boiling water for 3 minutes. Cool under cold running water and drain on kitchen paper.

4 Finely grate the zest from the remaining half of the orange and squeeze and reserve 4 tsp juice.

5 Drain off the marinade from the beef. Heat the vegetable oil in a wok or deep frying-pan until very hot, then stir-fry the beef for 1 minute to brown. Drain off all the oil.

6 Add the grated orange zest and juice, hot chilli powder, dark soy sauce, soft brown sugar and sesame oil. Stir-fry for 1 minute then transfer to a warmed serving dish and sprinkle the orange strips over the top. Arrange the boiled noodles around the meat and serve immediately.

Nick Carman

STEAK DIANE

Clint Brown

<u>Steak Diane originated in Australia where the use of fillet steak is obligatory for this quick dish. Nevertheless, rump steak would make a tasty alternative.</u>

PREPARATION TIME: 10 MINS
COOKING TIME: 15 MINS
SERVES 4

I N G R E D I E N T S

100 G/4 OZ BUTTER

1 SMALL ONION, VERY FINELY DICED

4 x 175 G/6 OZ FILLET STEAKS

75 G/3 OZ OYSTER MUSHROOMS,
SLICED

SALT AND GROUND BLACK PEPPER

1 TBLS LEMON JUICE

2 TBLS WORCESTERSHIRE SAUCE

PINCH OF CASTER SUGAR

4 TSP BRANDY

2 TBLS FINELY CHOPPED PARSLEY

1 Melt 50 g/2 oz of the butter in a frying-pan and sauté the onion for 2 minutes until slightly softened. Remove from the pan and keep warm.

2 Turn up the heat and fry the steaks for 1-2 minutes on each side until lightly browned.

SERVE WITH BUTTERED NEW POTATOES AND A CRISP GREEN SALAD.

A FULL-BODIED RED WINE WILL COMPLEMENT THIS MEAT DISH PERFECTLY. TRY AN ITALIAN BAROLO.

3 Add the remaining butter and mushrooms, return the onions to the pan and stir well. Season.

4 Pour in the lemon juice and Worcestershire sauce. Sprinkle in the sugar, bring to the boil.

5 Pour in the brandy and quickly ignite with a taper. Allow the flames to die out before stirring in the parsley.

SIRLOIN WITH WHISKY SAUCE

Complement the smooth texture of the creamy sauce by serving this dish with a crisp green salad and crunchy bread rolls.

PREPARATION TIME: 5 MINS
COOKING TIME: 20 MINS
SERVES 4

I N G R E D I E N T S

900 G/2 LB SIRLOIN STEAK ABOUT
2 CM/¾ IN THICK

SUNFLOWER OIL,
FOR FRYING

4-6 TBLS WHISKY

150 ML/¼ PT HOMEMADE BEEF
STOCK OR WATER

2 TSP GREEN PEPPERCORNS

150 ML/¼ PT DOUBLE CREAM

SALT AND GROUND BLACK PEPPER

3 Add the stock or water to the pan, then add the peppercorns and cream. Season and simmer for a few minutes, stirring continuously.

4 Stir the juices that have oozed from the steaks into the sauce. Serve poured over the steaks.

TIP

WHY NOT TRY FLAMING THE STEAKS? FLAMING BURNS OFF THE ALCOHOL FROM ANY SPIRIT, LEAVING JUST ITS FLAVOUR BEHIND. EITHER SPOON THE WHISKY OVER THE MEAT IN THE PAN AND IGNITE WITH A TAPER, OR HEAT IT IN A SMALL PAN OR LADLE, IGNITE THEN POUR OVER THE STEAKS. VERY HOT PANS, HOWEVER, WILL MAKE THE ALCOHOL EVAPORATE IMMEDIATELY, SO THERE WOULD BE NO CHANCE TO FLAME IT.

1 Trim the steaks of fat if desired and cut into 4 pieces. Brush a frying-pan with oil and place over high heat. When the oil starts to smoke, put the steaks in the pan. Fry for 3 minutes each side, lifting them now and again to stop them from sticking.

2 Spoon the whisky over the steaks and cook for a few minutes. Take the steaks out of the pan, put them on a plate and keep warm.

PORK STROGANOFF

Clint Brown

One of the best known dishes from Russia,
stroganoff is usually made with beef fillet.
Tender fillet of pork is just as successful.

PREPARATION TIME: 10 MINS
COOKING TIME: 15 MINS
SERVES 4

INGREDIENTS

800 G/1 LB 12 OZ PORK FILLET
1 TBLS OIL
25 G/1 OZ BUTTER
2 ONIONS, THINLY SLICED
2 TBLS BRANDY
250 ML/9 FL OZ SOURED CREAM
SALT AND GROUND BLACK PEPPER
CHOPPED PARSLEY, TO GARNISH
LARGE PINCH OF PAPRIKA

3 Increase the heat. Add a little extra oil and butter and quickly fry half the pork for 3-4 minutes or until lightly browned. Transfer to a plate and cook remaining meat in the same way.

1 Remove any excess fat from the pork and cut the meat across the grain into 12 mm x 4 cm/½ in x 1½ in strips.

2 Heat half the oil and butter in a large frying-pan and fry the onions over a gentle heat until golden brown. Transfer to a plate.

4 Return all the meat to the pan and pour the brandy over the top. Heat gently for 3 minutes or until the alcohol has evaporated. Add the onions, soured cream and seasoning. Bring to the boil, sprinkle with chopped parsley and paprika and serve immediately.

SERVE THE PORK STROGA-NOFF WITH BOILED RICE OR BUTTERED NOODLES.

TO COMPLEMENT THIS EASTERN EUROPEAN DISH, SERVE BULGARIAN CHARDONNAY — A DRY FULL-FLAVOURED WINE.

TIP

SLICED BUTTON MUSHROOMS ADD FLAVOUR TO THIS DISH — AND MAKE IT GO A BIT FURTHER TOO. FRY THEM AFTER FRYING THE ONIONS BUT REMOVE FROM THE PAN BEFORE FRYING THE MEAT. IF YOU DON'T HAVE ANY SOURED CREAM, IT'S PERFECTLY ALL RIGHT TO USE DOUBLE CREAM MIXED WITH THE JUICE OF ½ A LEMON. THE LEMON JUICE WILL SOUR THE CREAM.

INDEX